Kelber

Comprehension Mini-Lessons

Point of View & Fact and Opinion

by LeAnn Nickelsen
with Sarah Glasscock

NEW YORK • TORONTO • LONDON • AUCKLAND • SYDNEY
MEXICO CITY • NEW DELHI • HONG KONG • BUENOS AIRES

SCHOLASTIC
Teaching
Resources

I would like to thank the following people for this book:

my husband, Joel, and my twin children, Keaton and Aubrey, for encouraging and supporting me with the goal of writing this book.

my parents, Jim and Dolores Heim, for helping me with ideas and for all their support. Thanks Mom and Dad for creating the "Who Am I?" activity.

Virginia Dooley, my senior editor, for helping me become a more concise writer and for all of the writing opportunities she has given me.

Sarah Glasscock, my cowriter, and Sarah Longhi, my editor, who spent numerous hours checking over this book to make sure it was perfect.

Katie Lucarelle for her work on student samples.

my sister, Sherry DeVilbiss, for being a great, supportive friend. I know you really wanted your name to be in a book, so here it is (hahaha).

my education friends who have taught with me through the years. You know so much and have contributed so much time and effort. You know who you are!

Grapevine-Colleyville ISD in Texas for supplying me with resources and advice. Anne Simpson, your knowledge is valued by many. Thanks for the help with summarization and main idea.

—LeAnn Nickelsen

Cover design by Norma Ortiz
Cover art by Jason Robinson
Interior design by Sydney Wright
Interior illustrations by Teresa Southwell

Contents

Introduction

The *Comprehension Mini-Lessons* Series

National and state standards, and schools across the country require all students to master a set of reading objectives, with an emphasis on these key comprehension areas: main idea, summarizing, inference, cause and effect, point of view, fact and opinion, sequencing, and context clues. For me and the teachers I work with, teaching students to deepen their comprehension has always required several creative lessons for each reading objective to ensure that everyone achieves success. Customizing each lesson plan is a lot of work, and that's where this series of high-interest mini-lessons—the product of years of classroom lesson successes—comes to the rescue.

Each book in this series provides you with several different mini-lessons for each objective, which appeal to different learning styles and help you reach each and every learner. The mini-lessons include activities and real-world examples, so that students have fun learning the reading objective and find the skills they learn useful in their everyday reading and pertinent to their lives.

About This Book

This book presents lessons that teach students skills and strategies for understanding point of view and fact and opinion.

Point of View

There are three main points of view from which a narrative can be written: first person (one of the characters tells the story); third person (someone outside the story narrates); and omniscient (storyteller knows each character's experiences, feelings, and actions). Understanding how point of view shapes a story connects readers more deeply to the text. Students who can recognize point of view can determine the biases of the author or narrator, step into a character's shoes, make accurate predictions, and become more invested in the outcome of the story or passage.

Fact and Opinion

Facts are statements about things that have happened or are true. Opinions represent feelings and attitudes. Being able to distinguish between facts and opinions helps readers question the validity of a statement, respect diverse viewpoints and opinions, differentiate what can be changed and what cannot be changed, and use fact and opinion statements appropriately in their writing to persuade an audience.

How to Use This Book

You'll find five mini-lessons on point of view and five on fact and opinion with activities that stimulate different learning styles. I recommend teaching the lessons sequentially. The first lesson introduces the objective in simple terms. The subsequent lessons elaborate on the objective and offer students different skills to better understand it. The last lesson features the objective in a standardized test format which helps familiarize students with the test language and structure. A final project pulls the whole concept together. Projects are important because students can show creatively and elaboratively what they learned within the mini-lessons. They also get to share their learning with other classmates. Whenever students teach other students what they have learned, the learning becomes more cemented in their brains.

I suggest beginning your instructional unit with the point of view lessons first and then introducing fact and opinion. In this book, the point of view section is positioned first because it supports students' ability to understand opinions. If a student understands that there are several points of view to look at while reading and comprehending a story, then he or she will better understand opinions and be able to evaluate bias in writing.

—*LeAnn Nickelsen*

Young Adult Literature Resources

Here are some suggestions for young adult titles that support the objectives in this book:

Books That Look at Different Points of View

Cleary, Beverly. *Ramona Quimby, Age 8*. New York: HarperCollins, 1981.

Babbitt, Natalie. *Tuck Everlasting*. New York: Farrar, Straus & Giroux, 1975.

Dahl, Roald. *The Witches*. New York: Farrar, Straus & Giroux, 1983.

MacLachlan, Patricia. *Sarah, Plain and Tall*. New York: Harper & Row, 1985.

Books That Look at Fact & Opinion

Bunting, Eve. *Is Anybody There?* New York: HarperCollins, 1986.

Elmore, P. *Susannah and the Blue House Mystery*. New York: Dutton, 1980.

Fitzhugh, Louise. *Harriet the Spy*. New York: Harper & Row, 1964.

Rosenbloom, Joseph. *Maximilian, You're the Greatest*. New York: Dutton, 1984.

Point of View

Pointing Out Differences in Views

Opening the Lesson

❧ To introduce this lesson, I give each of my students a copy of the MAKE Meaning Model reproducible. This model will serve as a review of what they've already learned about point of view. It will also help them relate different points of view to their own lives. I take this opportunity to explain that as we explore point of view, we'll be looking at who's telling the story and from which perspective they're speaking. After going over the model with the class, I allow time for everyone to complete the model individually. (NOTE: the MAKE Meaning Model can be used to stimulate background knowledge for any lesson and can be used with any topic.)

❧ When my students are finished, I invite them to share one of the sections on their models with the rest of the class.

❧ Then I collect the models and keep them for a closing-the-lesson activity.

Teaching the Lesson

Part 1: Identifying Point of View in Literature

1. Use the Most Common Points of View transparency to introduce or review the three most common points of view—first person, third person, and omniscient. Then lead a discussion about the three literary excerpts shown on the transparency and ask students to identify from which point of view each is written. My students usually have little trouble identifying the *Twenty-One Balloons* excerpt as a first-person point of view; however, differentiating between third person and omniscient can be more difficult. I usually model my thinking for them in this way: *The first and second examples both use the third-person* he *or* them *to talk about the main character or characters. But I think that the second example,* From the Mixed-Up Files of Mrs. Basil E. Frankweiler *is omniscient because I know how both Claudia and Jamie are feeling, and I know what they're thinking.*

Objective

Students learn to differentiate among the most common points of view.

Materials

index cards, pens, paper

Reproducibles

MAKE Meaning Model, page 10 (Make 1 copy for each student.)

Most Common Points of View, page 11 (Make 1 transparency.)

More Point of View Examples, page 12 (Make 1 transparency.)

Comparing Points of View, page 13 (Make 2 copies for each student. Make 1 transparency.)

2. Then have pairs of students find examples of each different point of view from fiction they are reading. They can write a short excerpt from the book on an index card and on the back of the card write the point of view used. Let students share their examples and explain their reasoning with a partner. Encourage partners to bring any differences of opinion to the class's attention so that any confusion may be cleared up.

3. To check students' understanding, use the More Point of View Examples transparency. Read aloud the first paragraph, and then ask which point of view is used in it. Students should write their responses on a sheet of paper. When you say, "Show me," have students hold up their responses to show you what they wrote. Repeat the activity with the other examples. This is a great way to determine which students need more help.

Part 2: Taking a Broader Look at Point of View

1. Take this opportunity to review point of view as putting yourself in somebody else's shoes and forming opinions, feelings, and attitudes about a topic. Discuss these meanings to make sure everyone understands them.

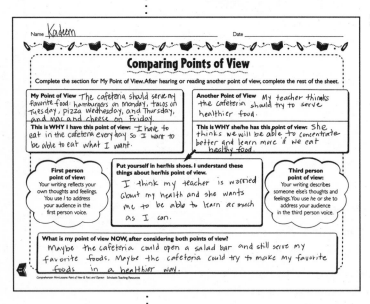

2. In this activity, students will learn more about the first- and third-person points of view by writing their own opinions, feelings, and attitudes about a topic and comparing them to someone else's—yours! Distribute the Comparing Points of View reproducible. Explain that they'll be discovering what their own points of view about a specific topic are. (NOTE: You should choose a topic and write your own response to it, such as the type of food served in the cafeteria, on the Comparing Points of View transparency.)

3. Share the topic you've chosen with students, and ask them to write three to four sentences describing their own viewpoints about the topic. They should include details to support their viewpoint in the second box. When they have completed the first two boxes, reveal the transparency with your own point of view and supporting details. Then ask students to write a brief summary of it, including the details, in the Another Point of View box. Give them time to "put themselves in your shoes" and to use their thoughts to complete the reproducible. Have

their responses to the topic changed, or have their points of view been strengthened? Show them how writing from their own perspective establishes a first-person point of view and writing to explain someone else's perspective establishes a third-person point of view.

Closing the Lesson

Use one or more of these activities to wrap up the mini-lesson.

✱ **Journal:** Ask students to add to the A, K, and E sections on their MAKE Meaning Model reproducibles now that they've had the opportunity to consider someone else's point of view.

✱ **Work at Home:** Let students take home the Comparing Points of View reproducible. They can ask family members to respond with their viewpoints on a topic. Decide on a topic before they do this. For instance, my class chose the topic of bedroom cleanliness.

Answers

Most Common Points of View, page 11: 1. Third person; 2. Omniscient; 3. First person
More Point of View Examples, page 12: 1. Third person; 2. First person; 3. Omniscient

MAKE Meaning Model

My topic of information: <u>Point of View</u>

Applying this topic to my life: How could learning about others' points of view and your own point of view help you become a better reader and a better friend? Why do you think you need to learn about this topic?

_____

_____

_____

_____

Knowledge I have about this topic: What do you already know about point of view?

_____

_____

_____

_____

Experiences I've had with this topic: Have you ever changed your point of view after having a discussion with someone who had a different point of view? What did that person say to change your point of view? How did you feel about it? Briefly explain what happened.

_____

_____

_____

_____

_____

_____

Comprehension Mini-Lessons: Point of View & Fact and Opinion   Scholastic Teaching Resources

Most Common Points of View

Point of view is the angle from which a story is told. It is the relationship of the storyteller to the characters and events.

Most Common Points of View

First Person: One of the characters tells the story. The storyteller uses the first-person *I* to tell his or her own experiences, thoughts, feelings, and actions. (KEY WORDS: *I, me, my*)

Third Person (also known as Limited Point of View): The story is usually told chiefly from the main character's point of view. Most of the books you read are probably written in the third person. (KEY WORDS: *he, she, it, her, his*, and so on)

Omniscient (also known as All-Knowing Point of View): The storyteller knows each character's experiences, thoughts, feelings, and actions. (KEY WORDS: *he, she, it, her, his*, and so on)

Examples of Point of View

Identify which paragraphs are told from the first-person, third-person, or omniscient points of view.

1. From *Maniac Magee* by Jerry Spinelli (Scholastic, 1990), page 76

So he turned and started walking north on Hector, right down the middle of the street, right down the invisible chalk line that divided East End from West End. Cars beeped at him, drivers hollered, but he never flinched. The Cobras kept right along with him on their side of the street. So did a bunch of East Enders on their side. One of them was Mars Bar. Both sides were calling for him to come over.

2. From *From the Mixed-Up Files of Mrs. Basil E. Frankweiler*, by E.L. Konigsburg (Yearling, 1977), pages 89–90

Claudia was furious. "The men who moved it last night hugged it when they moved it. There's all kinds of hugging."

She refused to look at Jamie again and instead stared at the statue. The sound of footsteps broke the silence and her concentration. Footsteps from the Italian Renaissance were descending upon them! The guard was coming down the steps. Oh, baloney! thought Jamie. There was just too much time before the museum opened on Sundays. They should have been in hiding already. Here they were out in the open with a light on!

3. From *The Twenty-One Balloons* by William Pène du Bois (Viking, 1975), page 39

It is funny that my trip has ended by being such a fast trip around the world. I find myself referred to now as one of the speediest travelers of all times. Speed wasn't at all what I had in mind when I started out. On the contrary, if all had gone the way I had hoped, I would still be happily floating around in my balloon, drifting anywhere the wind cared to carry me—East, West, North or South.

More Point of View Examples

Which of the following passages represents which point of view: first person, third person, and omniscient?

1. From *Number the Stars* by Lois Lowry (Bantam Doubleday Dell, 1989), page 3

> One of the soldiers, the taller one, moved toward her. Annemarie
> recognized him as the one she and Ellen always called, in whispers, "the
> Giraffe" because of his height and the long neck that extended from his
> stiff collar. He and his partner were always on this corner.
>
> He prodded the corner of her backpack with the stock of his rifle.
> Annemarie trembled. "What is in here?" he asked loudly. From the corner
> of her eye, she saw the shopkeeper move quietly back into the shadows
> of the doorway, out of sight.
>
> "Schoolbooks," she answered truthfully.

Point of view: _____

2. From *Missing May* by Cynthia Rylant (Bantam Doubleday Dell, 1993), page 47

> The day after May didn't come to us, Ob didn't get out of bed. He didn't
> get me up either, and from a bad dream I woke with a start, knowing
> things were wrong, knowing I had missed something vitally important.
>
> Among these, of course, was the school bus. It was Monday, and Ob
> should have called me out of bed at five-thirty, but he didn't, and when I
> finally woke at seven o'clock, it was too late to set the day straight.

Point of view: _____

3. From *The Lion, the Witch and the Wardrobe* by C.S. Lewis, pages 3–4

> He himself was a very old man with shaggy white hair which grew over
> most of his face as well as on his head, and they liked him almost at once,
> but on the first evening when he came to meet them at the front door he
> was so odd-looking that Lucy (who was the youngest) was a little afraid of
> him, and Edmund (who was the next youngest) wanted to laugh and had
> to keep on pretending he was blowing his nose to hide it.

Point of view: _____

Comprehension Mini-Lessons: Point of View & Fact and Opinion   Scholastic Teaching Resources

Comparing Points of View

Complete the section for My Point of View. After hearing or reading another point of view, complete the rest of the sheet.

My Point of View

This is **WHY** I have this point of view:

First person point of view:
Your writing reflects your own thoughts and feelings. You use I or to address your audience in the first-person voice.

Another Point of View

This is **WHY** she/he has this point of view:

Third person point of view:
Your writing describes someone else's thoughts and feelings. You use he or she to address your audience in the third-person voice.

Put yourself in her/his shoes. I understand these things about her/his point of view.

What is my point of view **NOW**, after considering both points of view?

A Mock Trial

(NOTE: This mini-lesson may take two class periods.)

Opening the Lesson

❀ I play four different types of music for the class, such as classical, pop, rock, and jazz. After playing a portion of a song, I ask my students to write about how the song made them feel—annoyed, relaxed, frustrated, energetic, distracted, and so on.

❀ After my students have listened to all the music, I pair them so that they can compare their points of view.

> **Tip** ....
>
> It's helpful to establish ground rules for the partners.
> ◆ Let your partner fully explain how the music made her/him feel.
> ◆ Don't interrupt.
> ◆ Don't make judgmental comments, such as "You like classical music? Yuck!"

❀ When pairs have shared their points of view, I then ask them to write about how they felt when their partners disagreed or agreed with them. Did their partners' points of view change their own points of view? Can they understand their partners' response to the music?

❀ Then we discuss their responses. Here are some questions I use to spur discussion: *Was it hard to suspend judgmental comments? Did you make yourself stay quiet when you wanted to interrupt?*

❀ At this point, I often share a personal story that illustrates how difficult it was for me to suspend judgment so that I could clearly understand somebody else's point of view. The story helps my students realize that everybody deals with this issue.

Teaching the Lesson

1. Point out that suspending judgments during reading, listening, and interactions with others can reduce the number of misunderstandings. It's essential to hear all sides before making a judgment. Explain that

Objective

Students explore how to determine the authenticity of a point of view by participating in a mock trial.

Materials

four different types of music, tape or CD player, paper, pens, scissors, bag

Reproducibles

Holding a Mock Trial, page 16 (Make 1 copy for each group.)

The Facts of the Case: *Lee v. Kris*, page 17 (Make 1 copy for each student.)

Defendant's Point of View, page 18 (Make 1 copy for each group.)

Plaintiff's Point of View, page 19 (Make 1 copy for each group.)

Judge's Job, page 20 (Make 1 copy for each group.)

this is what happens in our court system. The judge hears the details of an event from both sides—the defendant, who is accused, and the plaintiff who makes the accusation. After asking questions, reflecting on both points of view, and evaluating the law, the judge decides which point of view to favor.

2. Tell students that they'll have the opportunity to act as a judge, plaintiff, or defendant during a mini-trial. Divide your class into groups of three. To determine which roles students will play, have them draw numbers from a bag: 1–Judge, 2–Plaintiff, 3–Defendant.

3. Then hand out a set of reproducibles to each group. (NOTE: Remember that each group member receives a copy of the Facts of the Case.) Allow time for each member to read the reproducible that corresponds to his/her role. Then the judge should read the Holding a Mock Trial and the Facts of the Case reproducibles aloud to the group. The groups proceed by following the rules outlined on the Holding a Mock Trial and on the Judge's Job reproducibles. Circulate among the groups to make sure they understand the rules.

4. After the activity, poll the groups for their trial results. Be prepared—this discussion will provide good examples of learning to listen to other points of view!

Closing the Lesson

Use one or more of these activities to wrap up the mini-lesson.

✷ **Journal:** Ask students to record their feelings about the mini-trial in their journals. Do they think the trial and its outcome were fair? How did they feel when the opposing party or parties explained their points of view? How did playing their roles make them feel? How would they change the trial if they could? Why is it important to examine and understand all points of view before making a decision?

✷ **Verbal/Auditory:** Hold a class discussion and encourage students to share their journal entries. This usually sparks a spirited discussion.

Tip

If your class does not divide evenly into groups of three, place two plaintiffs and/or two defendants in a group. As an alternative, assign the following roles to your remaining students: court recorder or newspaper, radio, or television reporter.

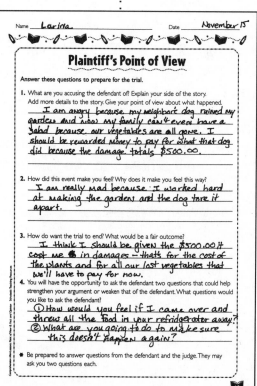

Holding a Mock Trial

These are the rules for the mock trial. The judge reads this page aloud to the rest of the group.

1. A group of three students holds the mock trial.

- One student is the Plaintiff, Lee. He/she receives the Plaintiff's Point of View sheet.

- One student is the Defendant, Kris. He/she receives the Defendant's Point of View sheet.

- One person is the judge. He/she receives the Judge's Job sheet and this sheet.

- (Nobody needs to represent the dog.)

2. Everyone reads The Facts of the Case.

3. Then the plaintiff and the defendant fill out their sheets. They will use these sheets to plead their cases. Remember, if you're Kris, you have to fight *for* your dog and *against* paying the fine. If you're Lee, you have to fight *for* receiving money for your damaged garden. If you're the judge, you have to decide who is right after hearing both points of views.

A NOTE TO EVERYONE: Be sure to listen well during the trial. Everyone will have the chance to ask one or two questions.

4. While the defendant and plaintiff fill out their sheets, the judge meets with the teacher to go over the Judge's Job sheet.

5. When the sheets are complete, it's time to start the trial!

Comprehension Mini-Lessons: Point of View & Fact and Opinion Scholastic Teaching Resources

The Facts of the Case

Lee v. Kris

Lee is the plaintiff. Kris is the defendant. Lee is complaining about the neighbor Kris's dog. Lee wants to be paid for the damage that Kris's dog, Rags, did to the garden. Rags has always stayed behind the fence in his yard. The dog has never hurt anyone before or caused any harm.

Then one day, while looking through the fence, Rags spotted a squirrel in Lee's yard. The squirrel began to tease the dog. Rags got upset, slid under the fence, and dashed around Lee's backyard, trying to catch the squirrel. In the course of the chase, Rags tore up the garden that Lee had spent hours and hours creating. Every plant in the garden was knocked over. Within a few days, all the vegetable and herb plants were dead.

Lee was extremely upset. The garden saves Lee about $500 in the spring and summer because the family eats vegetables from the garden and doesn't have to buy produce. Kris apologized but refused to pay $500 in damages to Lee. Kris claims that the damage was an accident and that no one was at fault.

Defendant's Point of View

Answer these questions to prepare for the trial.

1. What are you being accused of? Explain your side of the story. Add more details to the story. Give your point of view about what happened.

_____

_____

_____

_____

_____

_____

_____

2. How did this event make you feel? Why did it make you feel this way?

_____

_____

_____

_____

3. How do you want the trial to end? What would be a fair outcome?

_____

_____

_____

4. You will have the opportunity to ask the plaintiff two questions that could help strengthen your argument or weaken that of the plaintiff. What questions would you like to ask the plaintiff?

_____

_____

_____

_____

✿ Be prepared to answer questions from the plaintiff and the judge. They may ask you two questions each.

Comprehension Mini-Lessons: Point of View & Fact and Opinion   Scholastic Teaching Resources

Plaintiff's Point of View

Answer these questions to prepare for the trial.

1. What are you accusing the defendant of? Explain your side of the story.
Add more details to the story. Give your point of view about what happened.

_____

_____

_____

_____

_____

_____

2. How did this event make you feel? Why does it make you feel this way?

_____

_____

_____

_____

3. How do want the trial to end? What would be a fair outcome?

_____

_____

_____

4. You will have the opportunity to ask the defendant two questions that could help
strengthen your argument or weaken that of the defendant. What questions would
you like to ask the defendant?

_____

_____

_____

_____

✾ Be prepared to answer questions from the defendant and the judge. They may
ask you two questions each.

Judge's Job

The job of judge is difficult because you have to use your set of values, the law, and common sense to decide who will win the trial. Since you don't know the law, you will have to use your values and common sense to decide what will happen in this case.

There are many ways this trial could end.

❋ Lee gets some or all the money for the garden from Kris.

OR

❋ Lee doesn't receive any money. Kris doesn't receive any blame. Both have to pay court costs.

OR

❋ The judge can make a creative decision. (But don't be silly about this. Make your decision as real as possible).

You're in charge of making sure the trial goes in the following order:

1. Read aloud *The Facts of the Case: Lee v. Kris* to the plaintiff and the defendant.

2. Allow the defendant and plaintiff time to complete their point of view sheets.

3. Then call the court to order. Sit facing both Lee and Kris.

4. Call on Lee to stand and read aloud his or her responses to the Plaintiff's Point of View sheet.

5. Allow Kris to ask Lee one or two questions. Listen to Lee's response carefully.

6. Now ask Lee one or two questions to help you understand the situation better from Lee's point of view.

7. Call on Kris to stand and read aloud his or her responses to the Defendant's Point of View sheet.

8. Allow Lee to ask Kris one or two questions. Listen to Kris's response carefully.

9. Now ask Kris to answer one or two questions to help you understand the situation better from Kris's point of view.

10. Summarize both points of view aloud and make a decision about the case. To explain your position, you must also explain the reasons behind your decision.

Comprehension Mini-Lessons: Point of View & Fact and Opinion Scholastic Teaching Resources

What's the True Story of "The Three Little Pigs"?

Opening the Lesson

❋ I ask my class to tell the story of "The Three Little Pigs." I either call on volunteers or go around the room in order and have each student contribute to the story.

❋ I point out that we've only heard from the pigs' point of view. (In literary terms, the story is told from the third-person limited point of view.) We've never heard the wolf tell his side of the story. We've always assumed the wolf was the bad guy, but could it be that the pigs were the bad guys?

❋ Then I read aloud *The True Story of the Three Little Pigs* by Jon Scieszka and ask, *"How does this story compare to the traditional story you just told? What do you think of the new twist on the old story?"*

Teaching the Lesson

1. Have pairs of students use the Comparing Points of View reproducible to outline the surviving pig's point of view and the wolf's point of view in the Scieszka book. One partner can be the pig and the other partner can take the role of the wolf. Each student should fill out the "My Point of View" section and then complete the "Another Point of View" section after comparing viewpoints. Partners should work together to complete the final box. Who do they think really was guilty in the death of the two little pigs?

2. Set aside time for students to share their points of view with the whole class.

3. Now students get a chance to write their own "Twisted Fairy Tales." Before they begin, give them another example of how to "twist" a fairy tale. Summarize the traditional telling of "Jack and the Beanstalk." Then read aloud the "twisted" version "Jill and the Beanstalk" from *Newfangled Fairy Tales* by Bruce Lansky. (Or you can choose any of the other fairy tales in Lansky's book.)

Objective

Students write a familiar story from a different character's point of view.

Materials

"The Three Little Pigs" (any traditional version), *The True Story of the Three Little Pigs* by Jon Scieszka (Scholastic, 1989), *Newfangled Fairy Tales* by Bruce Lansky (Simon and Schuster, 1997), paper, pens

Reproducibles

Comparing Points of View, page 13 (Make 1 copy for each student.)

Twisted Fairy Tale Writing Rubric, page 23 (Make 1 copy for each student.)

4. Let students choose the fairy tale they want to twist. Some ideas are listed below.

Cinderella

Little Red Riding Hood

Sleeping Beauty

Goldilocks and the Three Bears

The Hare and the Tortoise

The Gingerbread Boy

The Princess and the Pea

Hansel and Gretel

Snow White

Rapunzel

5. Distribute the Twisted Fairy Tale Writing Rubric, review with students the assignment criteria listed on it, and answer any questions.

6. You might want students to take this piece of writing through the writing process (brainstorm, organize, rough draft, edit, and final copy). If so, review the steps in the process with them.

Closing the Lesson

Use one or more of these activities to wrap up the mini-lesson.

❋ **Auditory/Verbal:**
Encourage students to share their stories with the class. They may dress up as the character who is telling the story and disguise their voices.

❋ **Assessment:** As students read aloud their stories, you can use the rubric to grade their writing. After collecting the stories, look for punctuation and editing mistakes.

Big Red Riding Hood
A Twisted Fairy Tale by Nicole C.

Reddy is my name and riding my bike is my game. I live in a St. Louis, Missouri apartment next to the St. Louis Arch. Every time I look out my window, all I see is the huge arch which blocks the view of the Mississippi River and the country beyond that. I hate living in these cramped quarters and the busy, polluted, loud city. I have tried to escape several times on my red bike, but each time I've crossed the bridge that takes me to the peaceful country, my grandmother (Big Red Riding Hood is her nickname) would catch up with me and bring me back home. She can drive her little car very fast—faster than I can pedal—and I never made it into the country until one amazing day last summer.

You see, grandma is the type who fears anything beyond the city; at least that is what she tells me. She says that the country had wild, vicious animals that attack people. I used to laugh at that because the city has people that attack other people. But I lived with grandma, so I had to respect her wishes. Everyone who lived around us also respected grandma's wishes. She had an aura about her that put her on a pedestal. People were actually afraid of her. Everyone knew of her even though she hardly ever left the apartment. People looked at her as if she had done some heroic feat for them. I never understood what made her so special until the day I finally escaped.

One hot summer day, Big Red Riding Hood was not fast enough to stop me from following the rural routes that took me across the river. I jumped onto my bike and pedaled faster than E.T.'s friend. The view was so beautiful—the clear, blue sky, fresh smell of leaves, and cool breeze on my face. I was feeling total freedom as I pedaled my bike away from the busy city and into the calm country. I began to smell something so delicious that I became mesmerized and had no idea where I was going, but it was definitely towards the yummy smell. As I got closer, I realized the smell was of pumpkin muffins, my favorite dessert of all time. I was determined to find these muffins I was known for losing my mind when pumpkin muffins were near me. I had a craving that was out of control!

Finally, I was sure that I had reached my dream destination. I threw aside my bike and ran towards a huge, hollow tree just like the centerpiece tree at Animal Kingdom at Disney. I opened the door and heard laughter and music. Would you believe that there were more than 100 pumpkin muffins right in front of me with about 50 wolves surrounding them? I thought, "How can I discreetly get some of those muffins?"

1

Twisted Fairy Tale Writing Rubric

Student's name _____

Twisted fairy tale title _____

Based on the fairy tale _____

CRITERIA	Incomplete 0	Okay 1	Good 2	Outstanding 3

Assignment

1. The story is based on a familiar fairy tale.

2. The story is written from a specific character's point of view.

3. The main character is different from the main character in the traditional story. (The author gives a nontraditional viewpoint.)

4. The story is different from the traditional story.

5. The new story gives a creative twist to the traditional story.

Structure and Style

6. The story has an introduction, a sequence of three or four events, and a conclusion.

7. The story contains colorful details and language. The reader can visualize the story in his or her mind.

Presentation

8. The story is edited. (Spelling, punctuation, capitalization, and grammar have been checked and corrected.)

9. The story is at least one and one half pages in length.

10. The story is written neatly.

Things you did well:

Opportunities for growth:

TOTAL SCORE: _____ /30

Comprehension Mini-Lessons: Point of View & Fact and Opinion Scholastic Teaching Resources

Current Event Views

Opening the Lesson

✽ I begin this mini-lesson by reading aloud a newspaper article about an international event and allowing my students to discuss the article. (This mini-lesson can tie in easily to your social studies curriculum.)

✽ After the initial discussion, I point out that someone who lived in the country where the event occurred would probably have a different point of view about the event than someone in this country would. But I also emphasize that events in other countries can have an impact on Americans.

Teaching the Lesson

1. At this point, explain to students that there are first-person and third-person points of view expressed in newspaper and magazine articles. Factual articles are meant to inform, and they will always use the third person. Articles using the first-person convey writers' opinions and are meant to entertain or persuade readers.

2. Read aloud another newspaper article. Display the Current Event Point of View graphic organizer on the overhead projector, and show how to complete it. Model writing a summary of the article (who did what, where, when, why, and how). Then ask students to supply the important facts from the article to consider and record their answers.

3. Ask students what might be the viewpoint of someone from the foreign country discussed in the article. Then ask what a U.S. viewpoint might be. On the transparency, write your own first-person point of view in the adult's section. Ask students to write their own first-person points of view in their journals. Discuss their responses. You might want to point out that editorial writers often write in the first-person voice and reporters most often write in the third-person voice that represents the perspective of the newspaper.

Objective

Students assess different points of view based on a newspaper article.

Materials

variety of newspaper articles on international events, paper, pens, paper clips or stapler

Reproducibles

Current Event Point of View, page 26 (Make 1 copy for each student/1 transparency.)

4. Pass out copies of the Current Event Point of View reproducible, and have students complete it for homework. Encourage them to find newspaper articles about another international event. (Be sure to have some extra articles on hand for students who may not have access to a newspaper.) Students can get their parents or caretakers involved by asking them to contribute the adult's point of view. Tell them to attach the article to the completed reproducible so you can assess

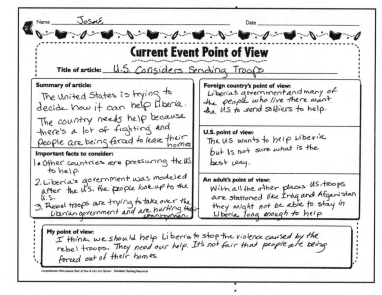

how well they were able to summarize the issue and express the point of view from a foreign and U.S. perspective.

Closing the Lesson

Use one or more of these activities to wrap up the mini-lesson.

❋ **Journal:** Challenge students to respond to this question in their journals: *Why is it important to look at an event from different points of view?*

❋ **Extension:** The day after students turn in their Current Event Point of View reproducibles, distribute a completed sheet to each student (make sure no one receives his or her own). Have them read the corresponding articles and viewpoints and then write their own points of view on the back of the sheets.

Name _____

Date _____

Current Event Point of View

Title of article: _____

Summary of article:

Important facts to consider:

Foreign country's point of view:

U.S. point of view:

An adult's point of view:

My point of view:

Comprehension Mini-Lessons: Point of View & Fact and Opinion Scholastic Teaching Resources

Test-Taking Format

Opening the Lesson

♣ For a quick review of first- and third-person points of view, I engage my students in a guessing game using a transparency of the Who Am I? reproducible on the overhead. I cover the clues and reveal them one at a time, challenging students to figure out who or what is speaking. As each line is revealed, my students write down their guesses. I tell them that a guess can only be changed once, so it's wise to wait until all the clues have been given.

♣ After we talk about the guesses and how the clues helped identify each speaker, I turn the discussion to point of view. I ask: *What point of view is used in all the clues? How do you know? What would you have to do to the clues to change them to a different point of view?* Then volunteers revise the clues to change the point of view to third person.

Teaching the Lesson

1. For this activity, students can choose their own mini-mystery stories or you can assign some from *Two-Minute Mysteries*. After reading the stories, students should write down who committed the crime and why they did it. Then direct them to write a paragraph from the point of view of a different character in the story. The paragraph should explain why the character thinks the crime was committed, his/her role in the event, and how it affected him/her. Emphasize that they can use either the first- or third-person point of view, but that they must use it consistently. Set aside time for students to read aloud their paragraphs.

2. Now that students have had the opportunity to review points of view, you can introduce them to the test-taking format. Distribute copies of the Point of View passages. Read aloud the first passage, "Listen to Me," and go over the answer choices. Think aloud about the question and the choices: *The president of the punch company does use the word* I *in the letter, but the president*

Objective

Students identify points of view in sample test passages.

Materials

Two-Minute Mysteries by Donald J. Sobol (Scholastic, 1967) or similar mini-mystery books, paper, pens

Reproducibles

Who Am I?, page 29 (Make 1 transparency.)

Point of View Passages 1 and 2, pages 30–31 (Make 1 copy for each student. Make 1 transparency.)

isn't telling the story. So A is not a good choice. Hannah is telling the story, and it is in the first person. B looks like the correct answer, but I'd better check the other choices. Both C and D state that the story is told in the third person, which is incorrect. The words I and my signal that the point of view is first person.

3. Let students complete the second question independently. Discuss their answers.

Closing the Lesson

Use one or more of these activities to wrap up the mini-lesson.

❋ **Assessment:** Have students complete the second passage, "Sea Horses in Danger," independently.

❋ **Writing:** Encourage students to write their own Who Am I? clues. You can compile them into a class book. Volunteers in my class typed their clues and answers (these can go at the back of the book). My students love looking through the book.

---

4. Who Am I?

❋ I am round.   *a circle*

❋ I come in different sizes.   *a ball*

❋ I have skin.   *a fruit*

❋ I need sunshine.   *orange, tomato*

❋ I am juicy and sweet.   *orange*

❋ I grow in a bunch.   *grapes, cherries*

❋ I grow on a vine.   *grapes*

Answers
Who Am I?, page 29: 1. dominoes; 2. clock; 3. bee; 4. grapes; 5. electricity; 6. fish
Point of View Passages 1 and 2, page 30: 1. B; 2. D; page 31: 1. C; 2. A

Name _____ Date _____

Who Am I?

1. Who Am I?

* I am a rectangle.
* People like me.
* I come in different colors.
* You can pick me up.
* You can count me.
* I have dots.
* I am a game.

4. Who Am I?

* I am round.
* I come in different sizes.
* I have skin.
* I need sunshine.
* I am juicy and sweet.
* I grow in a bunch.
* I grow on a vine.

2. Who Am I?

* People need me.
* I come in different sizes.
* Sometimes I make noise.
* You have many of me.
* I am mechanical.
* I have two hands.
* I tell time.

5. Who Am I?

* I am invisible.
* You use me every day.
* I can make things work.
* I can be dangerous.
* I don't mix well with water.
* I have a jolting personality.
* I come to your house in a wire and can light up your life.

3. Who Am I?

* I am tiny.
* I am noisy.
* My family is big.
* I like flowers.
* I can sting.
* I fly.
* I make honey.

6. Who Am I?

* I come in many sizes.
* I live everywhere in the world.
* There are many of me.
* I can see and hear.
* People eat me.
* I am a good swimmer.
* I can get caught on a hook.

Point of View Passage 1

Read the passage. Then circle the best answer for each question.

Listen to Me!

I took a gulp of the lemonade I had just mixed and almost choked. It was too sweet—and it didn't taste like lemonade at all. I tapped my mother on the shoulder. "This lemonade tastes terrible. Don't buy it anymore."

She nodded but continued to leaf through a cookbook. "Are you listening?" I asked.

The next week I discovered three new packages of the lemonade mix in the cabinet. Three! But I was so thirsty that I made a pitcher of the lemonade. I added less sugar this time. It was still too sweet. Yuuuuckk! And the lemonade tasted like pickles instead of lemons.

With a terrible taste in my mouth, I sat down to write a letter to the company that made the lemonade mix.

Dear People,
Have you ever tried drinking your lemonade? I'm sorry, but it tastes awful. To be honest, you should name it Pickle Punch instead of Sunny Lemonade because that's what it tastes like. Usually, no one ever listens to me, but I'm hoping that you will. I don't want your company to go out of business because you wouldn't listen to your customers.

Sincerely,
Hannah Garner

To my surprise, I received a large package from the company a few weeks later. Inside were different samples of drink mixes. In a letter, the president of the company asked if I would mind tasting its new drink mixes. "P.S. We'll listen. I promise," the president wrote. They did, too. The company even named one of the drinks for me—Hannah's Not-Too-Sweet Lemonade. Maybe you've tried it.

1. What is the point of view of this story?

(A) first person: president of the company

(B) first person: Hannah Garner

(C) third person: Hannah's mother

(D) third person: Hannah

2. Which words offer clues to the story's point of view?

(A) *president, company*

(B) *Hannah Garner, it*

(C) *mother, she*

(D) *I, my mouth*

Comprehension Mini-Lessons: Point of View & Fact and Opinion Scholastic Teaching Resources

Point of View Passage 2

Read the passage. Then circle the best answer for each question.

Sea Horses in Danger

Wading into the ocean, Bart scooped a glass jar into the salty water. He held the jar up to the sun. There they were—small creatures no more than a few inches long! Their curly tails swished back and forth as they swam. Bart got out a magnifying glass to examine the creatures. Their heads looked like horses' heads. He had done it! He breathed in a sigh of relief. He had caught—maybe saved—some sea horses.

The World Conservation Union, a group that protects nature, said that sea horses were in danger of becoming extinct. From Florida to the Philippines, fishermen supported their families by catching and selling sea horses. Some people ate the tiny fish. Others collected them. Bart had read that in China, sea horses were used to cure skin diseases and other illnesses. As a result, at least 20 million sea horses were lost each year. If something wasn't done to protect them, the only horses on the earth might be the ones on dry land!

Bart released his sea horses into the ocean again. He hoped that no one else would capture them. He hoped that the sea horses would be able to swim freely in the sea for the rest of their lives.

1. The point of view in this story helps the reader to—

(A) realize how sea horses act

(B) picture a Florida beach

(C) understand how Bart feels

(D) know what fishermen think

2. This story is told from—

(A) Bart's point of view (third person)

(B) the sea horses' point of view (first person)

(C) the World Conservation Union's point of view (third person)

(D) a Florida fisherman's point of view (first person)

Putting It All Together: POV Proved

Preparing for the Project

✿ For homework, have students work with an adult at home to create two different points of view on a topic that is easy to research. They should write down opinions representing both points of view and bring them to class the next day. Emphasize that they may use either a first- or a third-person point of view.

✿ Provide some possible topic statements so students and supervising adults will know what is acceptable. You may want the topic to be related to your curriculum—science, social studies, or language arts. Here are some topic statements that I've used in my classroom:

- The atomic bombs dropped on Japan were essential in bringing an end to World War II.
- Tiger Woods is the greatest golfer who has ever played the game.
- For the long term, the stock market is the best place to invest money.
- Water pollution is rapidly increasing in the United States.
- Air quality in the United States has improved in recent history.
- The reading test scores of American students in grades 4–8 have decreased in the past 10 years.
- Video games have a negative impact on students' academic learning.

✿ It's important that students choose a statement they believe can be supported or proven with available resources. Also emphasize that they should be genuinely interested in the statements they choose. Interest is the best way to motivate students for this project.

✿ (NOTE: If this assignment is too difficult for some students, have them work with partners.) Encourage them to take opposing views—one believes that preservatives in food increase cancer, while the other student believes that preservatives make longer and healthier lives possible.

Tip

Plan this lesson with your school librarian and computer specialist. This project is also an excellent way to get families involved in their children's work.

Objective

Students use research to support their points of view.

Duration

two to four days

Materials

a variety of resources including magazines, newspapers, books, and Web sites

Reproducibles

POV Proved Sample, page 34 (Make 1 transparency.)

POV Proved, pages 35–36 (Make 1 double-sided copy for each student.)

POV Proved Reflection Sheet, page 37 (Make 1 copy for each student.)

Introducing the Project

1. Have students share their point of view statements with the class. Ask them to choose two statements in case other students have duplicate statements.

2. Remind students that points of view that are supported by research are stronger and more credible than personal opinions. Display the example of the point of view on the POV Proved Sample transparency.

3. Show students how to complete a bibliography citation. Use the style adopted by your school district or the following standard format:

Rubel, David. *Encyclopedia of the Presidents and Their Times.* New York: Scholastic, Inc., 1994.

4. Now it's time for your students to do some research. Tell them that they'll be completing a POV Proved reproducible for one of their statements. Refer to the sample transparency to show them how to group the supporting details they've gathered into the following categories: facts, statistics, and real examples. Remind them to write information about each source on the second page of the POV Proved reproducible in the bibliography section. When they use a source, they should record the author, publication or Web site, and page number in the right column.

Assessing the Project

When the research is complete, ask students to fill out the POV Proved Reflection Sheet and staple it to the back of the POV Proved reproducible Ask them to share portions of their research with the class. You can extend this assignment by asking students to write papers based on their research. They may use the first- or third-person point of view.

Idea

I recommend asking parent volunteers to help with research in the library. You might even want to plan a day in the computer lab in order to pull articles off the Internet. Be sure to follow your district's Internet guidelines.

POV (Point of View) Proved Sample

Name **Mirella** _____   Date _____

POV (Point of View) Proved

TOPIC: Sleep Point of View Statement: *A good night's sleep improves memory.*		SOURCE Author/Page Number
FACTS	○ The more learning you do during the day, the more dreaming you'll do at night.	Jensen p.50
	○ You need 6-8 hrs. of straight sleep for really good memory the next day.	
	○ Best time of day to take in new information is just before sleep. It is remembered better.	Howard 504
STATISTICS	○ REM time makes up 25% of our entire night's rest.	Jensen p.80
	○ A large part of our sleep time is spent dreaming	
	○ Losing 2 hours of sleep at night might make it harder to remember things the next day.	Jensen p.181
REAL EXAMPLES	• TEST- Students who got more sleep the night before were more alert during class.	Jensen p.67
	○ University de Lille - France - found mind needs sleep to remember things that are harder to remember.	Jensen p.180

35

Name **Mirella** _____   Date _____

36

POV (Point of View) Proved, Page 2

Point of View Statement: *A good night's sleep improves memory*		SOURCE Author/page Number
EXPERT AUTHORITY	• By studying rats' brains, scientists learned that when rats are sleeping they are thinking or "rehearsing" what they learned.	Jensen p. 133
	○ Robert Stickgold -1998- Among rats, lack of sleep keeps the memory from growing.	Howard p.127
LOGIC AND REASONING	○ REM is a time of sleep in which learning is put together.	Jensen p.50
	• When you dream all of these ideas and pictures from your mind come together in strange ways.	Howard p.740
	• Sleep takes away stress. Less stress makes you more alert and able to remember more.	Howard, p.395
BIBLIOGRAPHY	Jensen, Eric. (1999) <u>The Great Memory Book</u>. San Diego: The Brain Store, Inc. Howard, Pierce J. (2000) <u>The Owner's Manual for the Brain</u>. Austin: Bard Press, 2nd Edition.	

34

Name _____

Date _____

POV (Point of View) Proved

TOPIC:

Point of View Statement: _____

	SOURCE **Author/Page Number**
FACTS	
STATISTICS	
REAL EXAMPLES	

POV (Point of View) Proved, Page 2

Point of View Statement: _____	SOURCE Author/Page Number
EXPERT AUTHORITY	
LOGIC AND REASONING	
BIBLIOGRAPHY	

POV Proved Reflection Sheet

1. Were you able to prove your POV statement? Explain why or why not.

_____

_____

_____

_____

2. What difficulties did you encounter during your research?

_____

_____

_____

_____

3. Place a checkmark next to the resource(s) you used to support your POV statement.

___ Internet ___ books ___encyclopedia ___ magazines/journals

___ other: _____

4. Complete this sentence: I got the most excited when I found the following

information: _____

_____

_____

5. What three things did you learn during your research (skills, information, something about yourself)?

_____

_____

_____

6. Now that you have completed your research, how do you feel about your original POV statement? Would you keep it the same, change the wording, or totally change the meaning of your statement?

_____

_____

Fact and Opinion

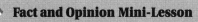

It's a Real Fact!

Opening the Lesson

❋ I read aloud *What's Smaller Than a Pygmy Shrew?* or a similar nonfiction book packed with facts about a subject I know my students will find interesting. As I read and show them the pictures, I have my students write down three facts from the book.

❋ Then I invite them to share their facts with the class. Once a fact has been mentioned by one student, no one else may use it again—this means they really have to be listening to each other!

Teaching the Lesson

1. Ask students how they recognized the facts in the book. After your discussion, read aloud the definition of the word *fact* from a dictionary. *Webster's NewWorld™ Children's Dictionary* gives the following definitions: "1. something that has actually happened or that is really true/I can't deny the *fact* that I was late./ 2. something that is said to have happened or is supposed to be true/Check to see if your *facts* are correct./"

2. Use the Word Web transparency to brainstorm synonyms for the word *fact*. Write the word in the center of the web, and record students' synonyms in the outer circles. Synonyms may include *reality*, *information*, *truth*, and *details*.

3. Then introduce them to a chant that will help them remember what a fact is: "It's a fact, it's a fact, it's a REEEAAAL fact." The key here is to extend and exaggerate the word *real* when you say it. As you repeat the chant, put your hands together and open and close them like you're opening and closing a book. Open and close your hands to the beat of each word. Practice this with students several times.

4. Now give students the opportunity to test their knowledge of facts. Read each pair of statements that follow. Have students identify which statement is a fact.

Objective

Students define, recognize, and give examples of factual statements.

Materials

What's Smaller Than a Pygmy Shrew? by Robert E. Wells or a similar book, a dictionary, newspaper articles, paper and pens

Reproducibles

Word Web, page 41 (Make 1 transparency.)

The Grand Canyon is America's most beautiful landmark.
The Grand Canyon is one mile deep in some places.

The Civil War was fought between 1861 and 1865.
The Civil War is the most fascinating war to research.

Remind students not to confuse facts with theories. A theory is a guess about something. Once a theory has been proven absolutely, it becomes a fact.

5. Pair students, and have them race to write down as many facts as they can think of in five minutes. They can use any of their textbooks for reference. Set your timer, and say, "Go!" When time is up, ask partners to draw stars next to any statements they're unsure about. Encourage them to share their starred statements, and let the entire class decide whether the statement is a fact.

Closing the Lesson

Use one or more of these activities to wrap up the mini-lesson.

✤ **Journal:** Challenge students to write a letter to a first grader explaining what a fact is and giving several examples. They may include some examples of statements that aren't facts.

✤ **Assessment:** Hand out newspaper articles to students. Direct them to read the articles and underline the facts. They should exchange articles with partners. Can partners find any additional facts in the articles? Have them use a different-colored pen or marker to underline additional facts. Make sure partners compare their work on each article. Do they agree about which statements were facts? In some cases, you may have to be the final authority.

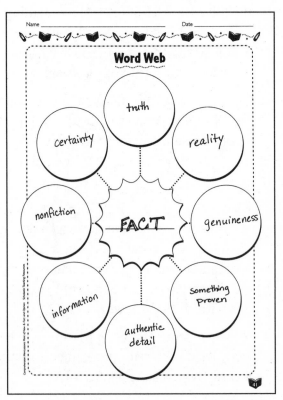

Word Web

Opinions Are Feelings and Attitudes!

Opening the Lesson

❋ Everyone has an opinion about *something*. Our opinions differ because people have different likes and dislikes. I give my students a chance to air their opinions by having them complete The Best! reproducible.

❋ I encourage each student to share and explain two opinions from their responses on the reproducible. This usually ignites a lively classroom discussion!

Teaching the Lesson

1. Read aloud the definition of the word *opinion* from the dictionary. *Webster's NewWorld™ Children's Dictionary* offers the following definitions: "1. a belief based on what someone thinks to be true or likely /We had different *opinions* about who started the argument./ 2. what someone thinks about how good or valuable a thing is /a low *opinion* of the movie/ 3. a judgment made by an expert/The judge wrote her *opinion* on the case./"

2. Introduce this chant that will help students remember what an opinion is: "Opinions are feelings and AAAATTITUDES." Really extend and exaggerate the word *attitudes*. As you chant, place your right hand over your heart and tap it with your fingers. Then open your palm. Tap your heart and open your palm to each beat of the chant. Practice this several times with students.

3. Brainstorm synonyms for the word *opinion* with the Word Web transparency. Write the word *opinion* in the center of the web, and record the synonyms that students volunteer in the outer circles. Synonyms might include *feeling, attitude, view, idea, inference, conjecture, supposition, theory, belief,* and *conviction.*

4. Tell students that noticing certain key words will help them identify opinion statements—if there is one opinion key word in a sentence, then the entire sentence is an opinion. Although there are hundreds of opinion key words, most fall into five categories: *like, good, nice, important,* and *think.* Explain that opinion words are synonyms or antonyms for the category words. They will see examples on the Opinion Key Words and Categories reproducible.

5. Distribute copies of the Opinion Key Words and Categories reproducible and display the transparency on the overhead. Model sample opinion sentences for the first category of like or dislike. Substitute synonyms in the sentence for the word *like: I like visiting Florida. I love visiting Florida. I adore visiting Florida. I enjoy visiting Florida.* Of course, someone else might have a different opinion about Florida. They might say, "I dislike visiting Florida. I hate visiting Florida. I despise visiting Florida."

Continue by asking volunteers to supply sample opinion sentences with synonyms for the other categories.

6. To help students become more familiar with key words that signal opinion statements, have small groups use the Opinion Word Category reproducible to brainstorm other words that fall into the categories you've introduced. Students may use words that have already been mentioned, but they'll only receive points for new words. Set a timer for five minutes, and say, "Go!" When time is up, ask groups to share their new words. Once a word has been mentioned, it cannot be mentioned again. Encourage students to add new words from other groups to their own lists. (Each student should have a separate reproducible to use for reference in future fact and opinion assignments.)

Closing the Lesson

Use one or more of these activities to wrap up the mini-lesson.

✽ **Verbal:** Have pairs of students discuss opinions. Let one partner explain how to tell if a statement is an opinion. Then the other partner can define what an opinion is.

✽ **Journal:** Challenge students to complete a RAFT writing assignment. Students get to choose the following:

R— <u>Role</u> they will play as a writer (Who will they be or represent?)

A— <u>Audience</u> (Who will they be addressing?)

F— <u>Format</u> of writing (In this case, it will be a persuasive paragraph or essay.)

T— <u>Topic</u> (What subject will I write about?)

For example, a student might write from the point of view of a pair of lungs (Role) to a cigarette company (Audience) giving its opinion in a persuasive business letter (Format) about the damage that cigarettes cause to the body (Topic). Allow time for students to share their work with the rest of the class.

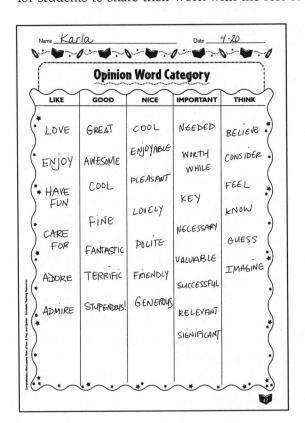

The Best!

Finish the statements below to show your opinions.

The best car is _____ .

The best sport is _____ .

The best color is _____ .

The best food is _____ .

The best drink is _____ .

The best song is _____ .

The best radio station is _____ .

The best television show is _____ .

The best school subject is _____ .

The best hobby is _____ .

The best animal is _____ .

The best season is _____ .

The best movie is _____ .

The best _____ is _____ .

The best _____ is _____ .

The best _____ is _____ .

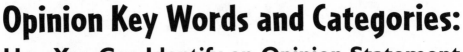

Opinion Key Words and Categories:
How You Can Identify an Opinion Statement

Use a synonym for each key word in a sentence that expresses an opinion.

1. *like* or *dislike*

Synonyms for *like*: *love, adore, admire*
Synonyms for *dislike*: *hate, loathe*

Model sentence: _____

_____

2. *good* or *bad*

Synonyms for *good*: *great, fantastic, terrific, stupendous, successful, generous*
Synonyms for *bad*: *rotten, terrible*

Model sentence: _____

_____

3. *nice* or *mean*

Synonyms for *nice*: *enjoyable, attractive, pleasing*
Synonyms for *mean*: *cruel, hateful, aggressive*

Model sentence: _____

_____

4. *important* or *unimportant*

Synonyms for *important*: *significant, necessary, relevant, needed*
Synonyms for *unimportant*: *useless, worthless*

Model sentence: _____

_____

5. *think*

Synonyms for *think*: *believe, feel, know*

Model sentence: _____

_____

Comprehension Mini-Lessons: Point of View & Fact and Opinion   Scholastic Teaching Resources

Opinion Word Category

LIKE	GOOD	NICE	IMPORTANT	THINK

Fact and Opinion Spinner Fun

Opening the Lesson

✤ I start the lesson with the two chants introduced in mini-lessons 1 and 2: "It's a fact, it's a fact, it's a REEEAAAL fact!" and "Opinions are feelings and AAATITUDES." I practice with my students until they can repeat the chants quickly and rhythmically.

✤ Then I read the statements from the Fact and Opinion Statements reproducible. I ask my students to determine whether each statement is a fact or an opinion. If it's a fact, they do the fact chant. If it's an opinion, they do the opinion chant. After I read a statement, I say, "Go" so that my students know when to start their chant. If there is disagreement about whether a statement is a fact or an opinion, we stop and discuss it.

Teaching the Lesson

1. In this activity, small groups of students will be playing a spinner review game. You'll need to prepare a reading passage for each group. I suggest using a chapter from a social studies or science textbook. Be sure to select a manageable chunk of text that best meets students' needs.

2. Show students how to fashion a spinner out of a pencil and a paperclip. Place the tip of a pencil inside a paperclip so the tip rests on the dot in the center of the spinner. (See the how-to illustration on the Fact and Opinion Spinner reproducible.)

3. To play the spinner game, players take turns reading two paragraphs from the passage. When a player has finished reading, he or she spins the Fact and Opinion Spinner and either states a fact from the passage when the spinner lands on FACT or gives an opinion about the passage when the spinner lands on OPINION.

4. Play continues until the group has read the entire chapter or assigned section.

Objective

Students play a spinner game to distinguish between facts and opinions and give examples of each.

Materials

pencil, paper clips, chapters from science or social studies textbooks or other content area texts

Reproducibles

Fact and Opinion Statements, page 50 (optional—for teacher's use)

Fact and Opinion Spinner, page 51 (Make 1 copy for each group.)

Closing the Lesson

Use one or more of these activities to wrap up the mini-lesson.

✱ **Journal:** After the game, ask your students to write the eight most important facts from the chapter and a paragraph that contains his/her opinion of the chapter's topic. Tell them to underline all the opinion key words in their paragraphs.

♣ **Verbal/Auditory:** Challenge your students to write an opinion about the spinner game. Emphasize that their opinions should be based on facts. Ask them to read aloud their opinions. Based on these opinions, can your class come up with suggestions about how to change or improve the game?

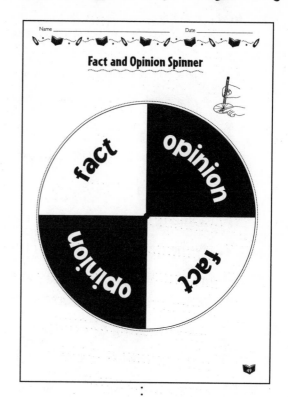

Name _____ Date _____

Fact and Opinion Spinner

Comprehension Mini-Lessons: Point of View & Fact and Opinion Scholastic Teaching Resources

To the teacher:
Read aloud each statement. Let students identify whether the statement is a fact or an opinion.

1. Plants need water, sunshine, and nutrients to grow. (fact)

2. My favorite subject is math. (opinion)

3. Our school library is open at 9:00 A.M. (fact)

4. Martin Luther King, Jr., won the Nobel Peace Prize. (fact)

5. Very little rain falls in a desert. (fact)

6. Montana is a great place to live. (opinion)

7. The heart rate accelerates during exercise. (fact)

8. In order to stand for many years, a house must have a firm foundation. (opinion—*Must* is an opinion word.)

9. I think it's going to rain tomorrow. (opinion)

10. *Charlotte's Web* is a fantastic classic story. (opinion)

11. Bees pollinate flowers. (fact)

12. Magnets attract objects made out of steel and iron. (fact)

13. Apples and blueberries make the freshest pies. (opinion)

14. The sun rises in the east. (fact)

15. Wheat is a grain that every person needs to eat. (opinion—*Needs* is an opinion word.)

16. Everyone should get eight hours of sleep at night. (opinion)

17. Swimming in a pool is more fun than swimming in an ocean. (opinion)

18. Apple juice is too sweet. (opinion)

19. Research shows that married couples can benefit from having pets. (fact)

20. Chocolate ice cream is the most delicious ice cream. (opinion)

21. Pluto is the smallest planet. (fact)

22. Mount Everest is the highest mountain in the world. (fact)

23. Planes fly faster than sound. (fact)

24. Airplanes are fun to travel in. (opinion)

25. Steel is a hard substance. (fact)

Fact and Opinion Spinner

Changing Facts to Opinions

Opening the Lesson

✿ In order to deepen students' understanding of facts and opinions, it's important for them to learn how to change a factual statement into an opinion statement. To do this, I read aloud *Is a Blue Whale the Biggest Thing There Is?* or a similar book to my students. As I read, my students record the facts they find most interesting. They use the following format: "The most amazing fact to me was . . ."

✿ After my students share what they wrote, I point out that in their statements they changed facts to opinions. We discuss how they accomplished this by using the phrase "The most amazing fact to me was . . ." to introduce the fact. I guide them to see that the opinion key words are *most amazing* and (in this context) *to me*.

Teaching the Lesson

1. Point out to students that they can change a factual statement into an opinion statement by adding an opinion word. If necessary, remind them about the five categories of opinion words from mini-lesson 2. You may want to display the Opinion Key Words and Categories transparency for students to refer to.

2. Next ask students to form opinion statements from facts. Think aloud and model the first example for them. *Fact: There are many different breeds of dogs. I think I can change this fact into an opinion by adding just one word. Here's one opinion: There are too many different breeds of dogs. Or, I could also say something like this: There are many different breeds of dogs, but the Welsh corgi is my favorite breed.*

Objective

Students turn a factual statement into an opinion statement using key words.

Materials

Is a Blue Whale the Biggest Thing There Is? by Robert E. Wells (Albert Whitman, 1993) or a similar book, reading passage from social studies, science, or literature book

Reproducibles

Fact Changer, page 54 (Make 2 copies for each student.)

Opinion Key Words and Categories, page 46 (Optional. Make 1 transparency.)

3. Write the following facts and sample opinions on the board.

   Fact: The moon travels around the earth.

   Sample opinion: The moon travels around the earth, but I'm confused about why it does.

   Fact: Big Bend National Park in Texas contains more than 800,000 acres.

   Sample opinion: Big Bend National Park in Texas must be gigantic because it has more than 800,000 acres.

   Discuss students' opinions and how they were formed. Have them identify the opinion word(s).

4. Then distribute the Fact Changer reproducible. Explain that you'll read a passage aloud. As you read, they'll write four facts from the passage on the reproducible. When they finish, students exchange reproducibles and rewrite the facts as opinion statements.

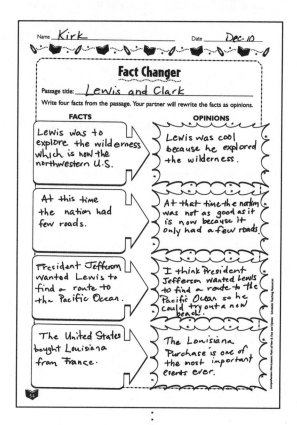

Closing the Lesson

Use one or more of these activities to wrap up the mini-lesson:

✤ **Journal:** Students write a short account of something that recently happened to them. While writing, they should make sure that they include facts as well as opinions. Have them underline the opinion statements.

✤ **Assessment:** Ask partners to check each other's work on the Fact Changer reproducible. The students who wrote the facts should look for opinion keywords within the rewritten statements.

Fact Changer

Passage title: _____

Write four facts from the passage. Your partner will rewrite the facts as opinions.

FACTS   ## OPINIONS

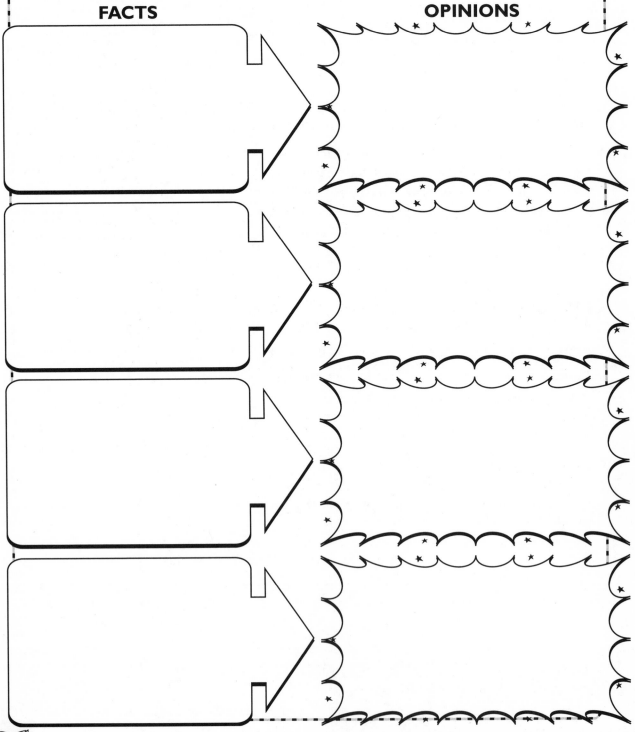

Comprehension Mini-Lessons: Point of View & Fact and Opinion Scholastic Teaching Resources

Test-Taking Format

Opening the Lesson

❋ Since my students have had practice in differentiating between fact and opinion statements, they should be ready to try their skills in a test-taking situation.

❋ I display the Sample Fact and Opinion Questions transparency, and ask my students to write the answers. Then we discuss each question and answer. I point out that questions and answer choices are typically phrased this way on the standardized test and I give some other phrasing variations that students may encounter, such as "Which of the following statements from the passage is NOT a fact?"

Teaching the Lesson

1. For this activity, students will use newspaper editorials. You may want to bring in a complete newspaper and go over each section in class. Describe each section, and ask students whether the section is fact-based or opinion-based, or a combination of both. Stress that editorials are opinions.

2. Pair students, and have each pair read an editorial together. Then they will write five facts and five opinions from the editorial in a T-chart. (NOTE: Some more sophisticated editorials may not offer many isolated facts and opinions. Tell students to record as many as they find.)

3. Partners will use the T-chart to write multiple-choice questions: one partner should write a fact question with four answer choices and the other partner should write an opinion question with four answer choices. Keep the Sample Fact and Opinion Questions transparency on the overhead so students can refer to the format and style of the questions.

4. Then have partners exchange and answer each other's questions. Remind them to read the article again.

Objective

Students choose correct fact or opinion answer statements after reading sample test passages.

Materials

paper and pens, editorials from various newspapers

Reproducibles

Sample Fact and Opinion Questions, page 57 (Make 1 transparency.)

Practice Fact and Opinion Test Questions, page 58 (Make 1 copy for each student.)

FACTS	OPINIONS
Teens and senior citizens cause more car accidents than any other age group. In some states, such as New Jersey, the legal driving age has been raised to 18. Only teens and people without licenses are required to take the written and road tests.	Adults seem to think teens are never old enough to drive. Every driver should be tested regularly for eye-hand coordination, reflexes, and agility.

Closing the Lesson

Use one or more of these activities to wrap up the mini-lesson.

✽ **Working Independently:** Let students practice answering multiple-choice questions with the Practice Fact and Opinion Test Questions reproducible. They should do this independently. Create more questions for students who need additional practice.

✽ **Assessment:** Compile students' fact and opinion questions in a binder. Give them the opportunity to select various tests to take. Keep an answer key in the back of the binder. And if your test-takers have questions about the test, they can go right to the source!

Answers
page 57 I. D; 2. A
page 58 I. B; 2. A

Sample Fact and Opinion Questions

Read the paragraph below. Then circle the best answer to each question.

Mrs. Kinkle's favorite book is *The Twenty-One Balloons*. She thinks the story really stretches the reader's imagination. It's a story about the most incredible voyage in the history of travel. Professor William Waterman Sherman left San Francisco on August 15, 1883, in a balloon. His intention was to fly across the Pacific Ocean. Three weeks later, the professor was picked up in the Pacific Ocean. He was found clinging to the wreckage of a huge platform that had been flown through the air by twenty-one balloons. As it turns out, Professor Sherman landed on the island of Krakatoa before he was found floating in the ocean. And, just after he left Krakatoa, the island was destroyed by a volcanic eruption. The book explains what the professor did for so long on this mysterious island, why he had some diamonds, and how in the world he got on that huge platform. *The Twenty-One Balloons* takes readers to a wonderful island where they will want to stay forever. Mrs. Kinkle believes that readers will want to read the book over and over again.

1. Which of the following statements from the paragraph is an opinion?

(A) Mrs. Kinkle's favorite book is *The Twenty-One Balloons*.

(B) The professor landed on the island of Krakatoa.

(C) Professor Sherman left San Francisco on August 15, 1883.

(D) It's a story about the most incredible voyage in the history of travel.

2. Which of the following statements from the paragraph is a fact?

(A) Professor William Waterman Sherman wanted to fly across the Pacific Ocean.

(B) She thinks the story really stretches the reader's imagination.

(C) Mrs. Kinkle believes that readers will want to read the book over and over again.

(D) *The Twenty-One Balloons* takes readers to a wonderful island where they will want to stay forever.

Practice Fact and Opinion Questions

Read the paragraph below. Then circle the best answer to each question.

I like to take a walk every day because it benefits me in many ways. For example, I feel more energetic after the walk. My doctor told me that this is because exercise pumps more oxygen throughout the body via the bloodstream. Blood is pumped throughout our bodies by our hearts. A vigorous walk makes the heart beat faster, and so it pumps more oxygen. I also enjoy walking because it helps me appreciate nature more. Those cute little baby squirrels that I see in the park are so quick and funny. The tall, green trees provide shade so that I stay cooler when I walk. Finally, I enjoy taking walks because it keeps me out of a kitchen full of yummy treats that are tempting to eat.

1. Which of the following statements from the paragraph is an opinion?

(A) My doctor told me that this was because exercise pumps more oxygen throughout the body via the bloodstream.

(B) Finally, I enjoy taking walks because it keeps me out of a kitchen full of yummy treats that are tempting to eat.

(C) Blood is pumped throughout our bodies by our hearts.

(D) A vigorous walk makes the heart beat faster, and so it pumps more oxygen.

2. Which of the following statements from the paragraph is a fact?

(A) My doctor told me that this was because exercise pumps more oxygen throughout the body via the bloodstream.

(B) Finally, I enjoy taking walks because it keeps me out of the kitchen full of yummy treats that are tempting to eat.

(C) The tall, green trees provide shade so that I stay cooler when I walk.

(D) I also enjoy walking because it helps me appreciate nature more.

Comprehension Mini-Lessons: Point of View & Fact and Opinion   Scholastic Teaching Resources

Putting It All Together: Fact or Fiction Flip Books

Preparing for the Project

❧ Cut 6 pages of construction paper into 4- by 12-inch sheets for the flip books. (NOTE: You may want students do this step later.) Create a sample flip book as a model for students. Also, display a calendar that includes the due date(s) for the projects.

❧ To review fact and opinion, I ask my students to write *true* or *false* after I read each of the following statements:

　1. Jupiter is the smallest planet in the solar system. (false)

　2. Ladybugs can sting people. (false)

　3. Cats have seven legs. (false)

❧ I emphasize that none of the statements is true. They aren't opinions, but instead, they fall into the fact category— they're facts that aren't true. For the purposes of this project, I call them fictional statements.

Introducing the Project

1. Explain to students that they'll be creating Fact and Fiction flip books on specific topics. Choose a broad topic and write down several subtopics that students could research. For instance, I've used the topic of the twentieth century for this project. I listed the following subtopics for my students to research: the Cold War, World War II, the Great Depression, the Dust Bowl, the Roaring Twenties, the Kennedy family, the moon landings, and Watergate.

Each student should select a different subtopic. This is a great way to cover your social studies curriculum—and students will be teaching each other.

Objective

Students create flip books containing fiction, facts, and opinions.

Duration

two to three days

Materials

calendar, paper and pen, self-stick notes (9 for each student), six 4- by 12-inch sheets of light-colored construction paper (1 set for each student), hole puncher, string, markers, scissors (optional), resource books (Enlist the help of your school librarian.)

Reproducibles

Student Project Sheets, pages 61–62 (Make 1 copy for each student.)

Guess and Check Note-Taking Sheet, page 63 (Make 1 or more copies for each student, depending on the number of flip books.)

Fact or Fiction Flip Book Rubric, page 64 (For teacher use: Make 1 copy for each student book.)

2. Display the sample flip book, and distribute the Student Information Sheets. Go over the instructions, and make sure everyone understands how to do the project.

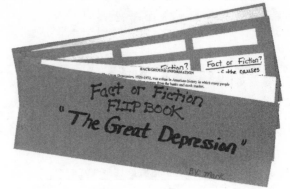

3. When the books are finished, ask small groups to take turns reading each other's books, guessing the answers, and checking to see if their answers are correct. Also have them complete the Guess and Check Note-Taking Sheet as they read each book (the reproducible gives them space to respond to three different books). Emphasize the importance of learning facts from each book. When a group finishes a set of flip books, collect them and pass them on to the next group. Continue this rotation until students have read all the books.

4. Hand out and discuss the Evaluation Rubric so students will understand how their books will be graded.

Assessing the Project

* **Verbal:** Ask students to tell what their favorite topic was. Which book did they learn the most from, and why?

* **Assessment:** After students have read all the books, collect their Guess and Check Note-Taking Sheets. Make sure they were filled out correctly. Then use the Evaluation Rubric to grade students' Fact or Fiction Flip Books.

Fact or Fiction Flip Book

Student Project Sheet

Follow these steps to make your fact or fiction flip book.

Step 1: Choose a topic to research. Take the time to research your topic well so that you can present all the information in an interesting way in your book.

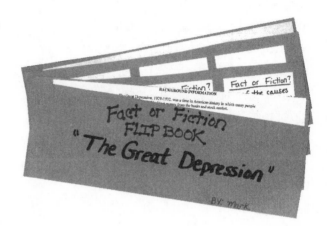

Step 2: Make a booklet with 6 sheets of 4- by 12-inch light-colored construction paper. Punch two holes along the left, narrow side of the booklet to create a spine. Thread string through each hole and tie it to bind the pages together.

Step 3: Here is what your book should contain:

Page 1 (cover page): Include the book title, your topic, and your name

Page 2 (background information on the topic): This page includes the most important information about your topic. Do not use information that you plan to put in your fact or fiction flips on pages 3, 4, and 5. This page will help the reader understand your topic better so that they can make appropriate guesses about your fact or fiction flips. Think of this page as a summary of your topic.

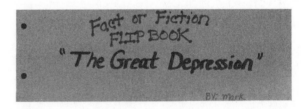

Fact or Fiction Flip Books

Student Project Sheet

Pages 3, 4, and 5 (fact or fiction "flips"): Place three self-sticking notes side by side on each page. The notes should flip up. At the top of each note, write FACT OR FICTION? Then write a piece of important information about your topic. It may be true (a fact) or false (a fictional statement that reads like a fact). Underneath each note on the construction paper, write the correct answer: FACT or FICTION. If the statement is fiction, explain why it is. Make sure your flips include a variety of facts and fictions.

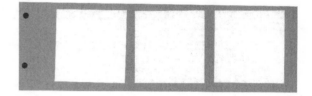

Page 6 (your opinion on the topic): To conclude your book, write a 6–8 sentence paragraph that states and supports a strong opinion you have about your topic. If you're having trouble coming up with an opinion that you can defend, use an opinion you've come across in your reading or ask an adult for help. Remember to support your opinion with facts. The more solid your argument, the more convincing your opinion will be!

Comprehension Mini-Lessons: Point of View & Fact and Opinion   Scholastic Teaching Resources

Guess and Check Note-Taking Sheet

Fact or Fiction Flip Book Topic:

Tally the number of correct guesses you made (*before* you flipped up the notes):

These are the most amazing facts that I learned from this book:

1.

2.

Circle one: I agree/disagree with this student's opinion about

because

Fact or Fiction Flip Book Topic:

Tally the number of correct guesses you made (*before* you flipped up the notes):

These are the most amazing facts that I learned from this book:

1.

2.

Circle one: I agree/disagree with this student's opinion about

because

Fact or Fiction Flip Book Topic:

Tally the number of correct guesses you made (*before* you flipped up the notes):

These are the most amazing facts that I learned from this book:

1.

2.

Circle one: I agree/disagree with this student's opinion about

because

Fact or Fiction Flip Book Rubric

Student's name: _____

Topic: _____

CRITERIA	Incomplete 0	Okay 1	Good 2	Outstanding 3
1. The cover page is neat and colorful and contains all required information.				
2. The background information gives a clear summary of the topic.				
3. The book presents the most important facts about the topic.				
4. The book contains a variety of factual and fictional statements.				
5. Notes are written neatly and precisely, and the information is accurate.				
6. The opinion statements are interesting to read and have facts to support them.				
7. Overall effort.				

Things you did well:

Opportunities for growth:

TOTAL SCORE: _____ /21